Lilli Josefine Wettke

612

Encounters with a stranger

AF280967

Lilli J Wettke

612

Poetry

Impressum

Bibliografische Information der Deutschen Nationalbibliothek:
Die Deutsche Nationalbibliothek verzeichnet diese Publikation in der Deutschen Nationalbibliografie; detaillierte bibliografische Daten sind im Internet über http://dnb.dnb.de abrufbar.

Lektorat: Isabell Wincher, Lena Parent, Alicia Lebkiri
Korrektorat: Lilli J Wettke

Verlag: BoD · Books on Demand GmbH, In de Tarpen 42, 22848 Norderstedt

Druck: Libri Plureos GmbH, Friedensallee 273, 22763 Hamburg

ISBN: 978-3-7597-8638-8

Contents

Introduction

Mesmerizing, alluring, dazzling

People change, but some were never good

-Empty phrases

L is for love

-Elements of love
- The fire motive – wooden puppet turn your-
self
-An evening at the beach
- A letter
- Do you still think, or do you already feel?
-Cursed

eloquent

-Do I understand that right?
-Optimistic philanthropy, but...
-The blindness of being able to see
-Butterfly effect
-Language is a playground for the rich
-Substance
- Thought thoughtless thoughts
-The complexity of being complex

A curse worth envying

-Pretty stones
-Caught in between two worlds

To be seen metaphorically

-Stolen wealth
-Roses have thorns
-I don't know
-Colouring the sky
-Survival and Death
-Arrogant

Words, many of them, my heart, my soul

-Antithetically
-Words
-From me for you

Of what I left behind

-Everything is great!
-Parched
-Do I love you?

For those,
who want to grow.
Sometimes you have to look back,
to recognise the string
that keeps you in the past.
It often takes time,
to find a pair of scissors,
but when you succeed,
then it is the greatest proof of courage,
to cut the thread.

For those
whom I love.
Here's to a wonderful future together.

Encounters with a stranger- a self-reflection

I find it difficult to write about myself.

I mean clear words, unpoetic, unambiguous,
clear words, no cryptic allusions.
Poetry gives me a protective shield behind
whose ambiguity and individuality I can hide,
cower behind, because each individual person
interprets my works in a different way, based
on their own experiences, values and views. In
my poetry I often turn my innermost self out-
wards, but in a way that leaves a lot of room for
interpretation. At the end of my texts my deep-
est feelings often lie unprotected, but this is
only recognizable to me. I am honest, brutally
honest. Anyone who reads my texts has a free
view of the landscapes of my soul, but some will
see a sea, others a hilly landscape, others a big
city.

It is hard for me to write down clear words
about myself on paper, and I don't know if this
is because I barely know myself, or because I
know myself too well. Sometimes everything in

me cries out to show me as I really am, but then I think about it, weigh up the consequences, and choose poetry.

Sometimes everything in me cries out to show me as I really am, but then I realize that I'm not just one person, I'm many people, there's no blueprint for people because we're so complex that there's not just the one reality of our personality.

I think I get to know myself in a whole new manner every day.

Every day I'm me, but that doesn't necessarily mean I'm me in the same way I was the day before.

I think with each day that we get older we acquire new views and new facets. We get to know ourselves and the world in a new way and learn to look at everything from a new perspective. Today I am the Lilli I am today; but also who I was yesterday and who I was three years ago are still a part of me.

These parts are views that influence, shape and strengthen my personality, they are experiences, feelings and perspectives that shape my view of the world, my opinions and my existence.

I consider myself an extremely self-reflected person who knows herself fairly well, because I am one of the few people who actually takes the time to understand me. Just because I am me does not mean that I can always understand my feelings and actions at first sight. I feel them, I carry them out, yet they are partly as surprising to me as they are to the rest of civilization.

I have learned to take the time to understand myself, to feel and validate my feelings, and to adjust how I deal with them to how I perceive them as healthy and good. I accept each of my feelings, take a look at them and not hold onto them. I let them go, let them fly like a bird. If they stay, I greed them with open arms, if they leave me, I let them go.

Having realizations about myself in my head is

not always a nice feeling, but it is a positive one throughout, because it means that through my self-understanding I can validate my emotions, and learn to deal with them.

I find it much harder to reflect outside of my head, because it is tied to factors outside of myself, to factors that I am unable to control.

Even though I accept myself on the full emotional spectrum, it is also deeply ingrained in my mind that other people judge me. I have always been used to being judged, which is why it is always too difficult for me to dismiss this worry. Before I speak a truth about myself that is not lapidary, that makes me potentially vulnerable, a fear of indescribable strength that is difficult to master and that I am not always able to overcome appears in me.

Still, when I finally force myself to carry my innermost-self outwards, when I hear the words that once formed in my head outspoken, it is both an incredibly captivating and an incredibly liberating feeling for me, it is the expression of boundless beauty, because it means trust.

When I talk to a person about things that make me myself, about my feelings, about my undisclosed qualities, about my ideas, desires and dreams, that is probably the greatest proof of my love and my trust that I can give.

I only get those concessions from the people where my heart says it feels right. What matters is not how long, or how well I already know the person, but how secure I feel with them. To all those, who have already seen my tears, to all whom I have dreamed openly, to all before whose eyes I have also talked about unrealistic things, to all whom I have let hug me; I love you! You mean the world to me and now you know *how* important you are to me.

When I express my thoughts and feelings in the form of words, it is both an incredibly captivating and an incredibly liberating feeling for me.

On the one hand, my words became an irreversible reality from the second they left my mouth, crossed the threshold of my lips, and on the other hand, they finally became an irreversible, heard reality.

Not only do I hear them, but also other people. Never again will these words, these insights about myself belong solely to me. At the same time, I find this incredibly frightening and liberating.

It is not only the fact that I hear my statement spoken out loud for the first time, but also that others do the same. I am unable to undo their hearing, and I cannot influence their reaction, but what I can do is trust. I can trust that I will encounter love and kindness, that I will be understood, and maybe with myself I can inspire others.

I can hear other perspectives, and I can like them, or dislike them, but I always broaden my perspective, my horizon, in every way.

I am unable to make sure that other people's views of me will not change, but who says that changes just have to be negative? I cannot control how their thoughts about what I said begin to form.

Furthermore, if I'm honest with myself, I know that this is constantly the case anyway. Every day, we are all different people, and perceive each other in different ways. One sentence I say, which may seem perfectly lapidary to me, can completely change another person's view of me, and the world moves on.

What I want to say is that we have no control over how people see us, or don't see us, no matter how much we open up or hide ourselves, so we can calmly give ourselves the chance to be healthy and open with ourselves, and not cower behind a wall of lapidary.

Let's just start being ourselves and show our true faces to the world.

I believe the strongest form of my engagement with myself is my writing.

This is probably also where my fear of putting my innermost self on paper comes from, because through my ink on the paper of my notebook it becomes not only real but also eternal. It becomes eternal and above all much more personal, because my words are all I have. My words are my art, my words are my soul, my words are my home, my words are my heart, and my words are my being.

Although it is incredibly difficult for me to put on the pen, to let the ink sink into the paper, even though I sometimes fear it, it is at the same time probably the most important thing I have ever done. By formulating the thoughts that are in my head into words, I force myself to give them structure. I force myself to arrange them and thus let them unfold to their full potential.

I think my writing is the highest form of my self-acceptance.

People change other people.
That is general.
But some people change other people more
than others do.
Once when I stood in front of a mirror,
I saw a stranger looking back.
I was not looking at myself.
That was not me.
I was changed, and I was taken from me.

See how some plants look nothing alike with
their sprouts?
I took the little that was left of me,
and I grew.
I was never able to be the person I was before.
However,
while growing,
a new me was created.
It has a few similarities,
but regarding carefully,
it is nothing like the person I used to be.
I am a mosaic.
Little crumbled pieces that can be put together
multiple ways to create art.

"Some people themselves are art <3"
-Isa

Mesmerizing, alluring, dazzling

Nostalgia

My favourite colour is evening red.

It symbolizes the farewell of a past day and the beginning of a new night.

A day brings a lot of beauty with it, but it has to come to an end at some point. In the evening red, thoughts get lost. In the evening red, past and future blend into a form of wonderful present.

Evening red is a form of nostalgia, which is hard to beat in its beauty. Evening red is the rose among all the grass, the gold among all the grains of sand, that you among all the mes'. It is the dawning of an old love in view of the fact that a new one is to come. Evening red is a beautiful feeling. A feeling that is capable of germinating so many other emotions if you allow it.

When I look into the evening red, I feel enough peace to be able to think about everything. I am like the evening red. I am the present, caught as an intermediate state in the midst of the waves that are raised by the past and the future.

I am tangible and I am peace.

I do not know what lies ahead for me, I do not know what the night may bring, but I will not be able to escape into the light of day forever, for it will continue to fade and turn into evening red.

To what is yet to depart, to uncertainty, to all the beautiful adventures!

A time travel

I am taken in by the charm of old things.

Reading old books, skipping trough their yellowed pages has so much elegance.

Carrying a pocket watch like an old days gentleman reminds me of the charm of the forgotten times.

Touching something old is like touching history.

Antiquities are like a preservation of long-gone times.

Browsing through old novels is like travelling in time.

It is a preserved perspective, a long-forgotten dream, a sunken wisdom.

I am taken in by the depth of old things.

Romanticised

I am a philocalist.

I see the beauty in every little detail, and I admire even the smallest things.

I wish that everyone would be able to see the world through my eyes at least once, because it makes our society, our world, seem so much less horrible and cruel.

I am a philocalist,
I see every little detail, that is why I am never bored.

I can sit on a bench for hours just noticing the bees on the uncountable flowers, seeing the little bubbles of the water, watching a child helping an elderly lady picking up her book from the ground.

I also see the people around me, running around fast and stressed, hoping that even when I become one of them I will always take a moment to slow down and practice the simple art of noticing.

They do not see the two pigeons sharing a piece of crusty bread, they do not have their eyes on the tiny fly walking on the leaf of the tree, of which branch hangs right next to me.

I am a philocalist, and my brain just seems to be romanticising life around me.

I do notice the terrible sides of our society, because I hear so much about them. I see them and I know they are there. I know they are real.

However, from the second I set my foot on my doorstep all I see is peace and beauty. I am reminded that good things still exist and I am so deeply thankful for that.

It is a kind of peace and beauty not everyone sees, because they are the tiny things.

Every little microcosmos, with its own unique way of symbiosing with its surroundings.

Every little perfect microcosmos working so seamless.

Every little perfect microcosmos helping to form a perfect macrocosmos.
Nature functions under its own laws that none of humankind are ever to understand, thus unable to control.
In nature, everything that is supposed to be happening is going to happen in a certain way, at a certain time.

That is what I believe in when it comes to humanity. Humans are animals, humans are nothing but nature in denial of itself; in denial of their own beauty.

I personally do not fully believe in determinism, but what I do think is, that when something is supposed to happen, it will, if you just let it be. In my opinion humans are able to make decisions in life, with their own reasonable mind, but if we would just let it be, if we only listened to the feeling in our stomachs, I think there could be a form of fate.

Me as a person, I am as much of reason, as I am not.

Sometimes, things just depend on the situation.
After all, everything that is set to happen will somehow happen in the way and at the time it is supposed to.

Everything will fall into place, if you just let it be and refrain from pushing it so hard.

Two opposites, hugging

The ocean is roaring,
a beast,
a queen,
a slave.

The ocean is strong,
The ocean is to be respected,
majestic.

The ocean is soft,
The ocean is weak,
alive.

The ocean is hugging the clouds,
horizon.

Pink, blue, puffy clouds,
dark, roaring, deep ocean,
two opposites,
hugging.

Two opposites,
but one.

Two opposites,
but none.

The liveliness of clouds,
the deathly depth of the ocean.

They are different,
but they love one another.

Stone-soft

You are soft as stone,
Stone-soft.

You are the softest person I know.

Life is always hard on the stone,
so long until it crumbles and crumbles,
so long that it is unable to bare the pain any
longer,
so long till it crumbles and crumbles and turns
into sand.

Life makes the stone show its real soul.

The stone pretends to be the hardest,
but facing life,
it is forced to show how soft its soul is in real-
ity.

You fight like a solider,
Claw like a bear,
when you really are a stone,
soft.

When you really are a stone,
hurt.

You are a stone,
soft,
and in the need of
love.

Urbanized nature

Tiny houses,
one next to the other,
they all look alike.

A brutal desert of boredom.

Branches,
leaves,
the smell of wood.

A wide view of freedom.

They tried to bring nature here,
here in the city,
where the howling of wolves,
is the browsing of a car engine.

They tried to bring nature here,
they tried to bring beauty here,
but they are taming the branches,
cutting the leaves,
and you are unable to smell the wood
under the car fuel.

They tried to bring beauty here,
but they tried to urbanize it.

They Tried to tame it,
they tried to control it,
and by cutting the leaves,
they cut off the beauty,
they cut off the freedom,
they cut off the perfection.

Master of change

The shallow waves,
they caress the stones on the beach.
So tender,
So sweet,
So formative.

Steady drop hollows the stone,
The love of water,
Master of change.

Perfection

Flowers bloom,
sun shines,
bees fly through the warm breath of air.

I inhale, I exhale,
I glance at ladybugs in the sunshine,
I look at flowers holding their heads up against
the light,
I watch butterflies dancing trough the fresh
breeze.

It is peaceful, I am at peace.

I know I should not be.

I am reminded by the sound of an airplane,
roaring,
leaving lines, marks, scars in the flawless sky.

But I am carelessly at peace.

I am carelessly at peace whilst being sur-
rounded by perfection.

Nature's perfection lays in the fact that it is
not.

I would like to take this rule,
and apply it onto people.

A stranger

A fire small and tiny,
killed by the wind.

An act of kindness from a stranger,
makes it live at ease.

Nothing still to see of that,
the fire big and strong.

But still the strangers fault it is,
that how far we've come.

The clouds in my head

A towel in the sand,
a glass of red wine,
the browsing of the ocean in my ear.

The sand in my hand,
my head in the clouds,
and the clouds in my head.

Watching waves,
slowly escaping reality,
The sound of a stone,
Landing on the water surface.

The sound of freedom.

People change, but some were never good

(Trigger Warning! This chapter contains graphic details of sexual violence and emotional abuse!)

Putting a spin on: Stolen wealth

I once was the richest person on this planet.

I have had everything until they entitled themselves to take it.

One day, life decided to come up to me and take my everything.

I once was the richest person on this planet, but then I met that woman.

I met that woman, and I was happy.
She seemed to be so flawless, she seemed to understand me. I felt like I finally got to know someone who got me, who was like me.

I thought that fate was finally on my side, I thought I was finally introduced to someone to whom I was so alike that they would understand me. I thought I finally found someone to whom I was so alike that they would not call me a freak for being myself.
I was in seventh heaven, and I spent so much

time with her that we grew close like family, actual family. Family as in the original meaning of "blood runs thicker than water". It used to say that the connection between friends made by blood-brotherhood, the connection with people we choose are much thicker than the water of birth that connects us to the family given to us by chance.

And you, you were family. You were my family, and until this day I am unable to understand why you did what you did.

I was lulled in by her presence, in a platonic manner, but that should not make one underestimate the intensity.
I loved her as my dear friend, as my platonic soulmate so I was blinded.

It started of plane simple, with her slowly reducing my other social contacts up until the point where there was just her. Just her and me. Just us against the rest of the world.
At least you made it seem like that... didn't you?

I became dependent on her without even noticing it to the slightest.

I felt like everything was finally getting better and better for me. I never really had a friend before, you know.
But in reality, in reality everything was getting worse and worse.

I would like to use the metaphor of me being trapped under her fingertip.

Physically, I would have always been able to escape until this point, but mentally... in the state of mind I was in I would have asked anyone "escaping from what?"

I believe, looking back the most soul crushing thing is, that I was told. That I was told that she was a terrible influence and I wholeheartedly protected her.

I do not blame myself, not anymore, but how? How could you do this to me, knowing how much I loved you, knowing that I would throw myself between every accusation against you.

One day she asked me that question, which I
am unable to forget even today.
I remember how it took the last bit of my free
will to answer how I answered, but you did not
like that, you did not like me saying no, didn't
you?

Well, in fact you did not care.

She did, what I told her not to do and without
my consent she stole all my wealth.
She stole my wealth and after she was done, she
said those words that scarred my heart to today.

I remember her looking out of those eyes I
thought I knew so well, that I loved so much,
and I remember those words coming out of her
mouth.

"The next time we proceed!"
I remember not sleeping that night thinking of
my stolen wealth whilst thinking that I stole it
myself.

I remember not understanding what was done to me, I remember my soul being crushed to bits and pieces and I remember being confused, not understanding why I felt like I felt.

I only then learned what the word manipulation meant and something in me clicked.
I only then learned what the word abuse meant and something in me clicked.

But the damage was done, the damage was irreparable, so I kept on loving her.

I wanted to make everything right, to not lose my love, to not lose my friend.

I strongly believed that she was a good human being so I went up to her again, telling her what she had done.

I gave you a chance, I really wanted us to be us again, how stupid of me to believe that this was actually a possibility.

I told her what she did to me and all I wanted

was an apology. All I wanted to hear were the words "I am sorry", was that too much to ask for?

I desperately pleaded for an apology I have never gotten and with that she made my good faith in people crumble and crash to bits.

She took that baby deer, a replicate of innocence and she slaughtered it brutally in a beautiful forest on a mild summer night with the branches of the trees dimming the moonlight.

I was the happiest person on this planet, but then I met that woman.

When she stole my wealth I thought my life was over but I kept on living.
I did not want to and I tried not to but unfortunately it was my fate to live.

It took the longest of time, but as she killed that baby deer a lion was born. It was weak and small. It was weak and small and needed care, but nobody was there, so I cared for it.

As times went by the lion grew and alongside did my wealth.

I am now again the wealthiest person on this planet and I am protected by a lion.

I will always be the wealthiest person on this planet, because nobody is going to take away my smile ever again.

That is a promise I gave to myself and the lion.

The pain in your eyes and the pen firmly in your hand, you still somehow manage to make everything sound beautiful.

A lapidary meaningfulness

Holding on to something is good, but holding on to something hurts, sometimes, most of the time, always, often.

Holding on to being held on to something.

Letting go and yet you are held on, because the memory of being held on is not so easy to shake off.

Holding on made her shudder, holding on does not make her fall asleep with fear at night and yet holding on is good for her, nevertheless holding on is healthy for her.

Holding on to holding on to something is not.

Holding on to something is strange for her, because holding on and holding on to holding on to something made her sick, yet holding on has healed her and given her a sense of security when she was at the very end.

Holding on is confusing because it is a neutral word without being neutral. Holding on and holding on to holding on outweigh each other. They are good and bad and thus neutral.

Holding on to something says far too little about its true meaning because holding on to something is so emotional, contrary to the lapidary sound of holding on.

The calm before the storm

The calm before the storm.

She likes to look at the sea. Often, she just stands there, with her bare feet in the cold sand and the blowing wind in her hair.

There is a certain smell that heralds the calm before the storm.
The breeze in her nose sounds like the sea's last cry for help before the storm swallows it.

She often sits there, on a dune, her dune, smelling this very smell and listening to the sea's painful screams.
The sound calms her, gives her a sense of home, of secrecy.

Now she lies there, twisted in herself.

Her body is in most places as blue as the sea. Red blood flows from her nose and from the cut left by his knife.

She had felt the calm before the storm on her way home, had rejoiced at the secrecy it gave her. She was bouncing. Only five minutes to get home.

And now she lies here, one hour later and she is still five minutes away from home.

The calm before the storm is gone, for the storm had broken loose.

Now she understood the sea, and why it was screaming.
Now she lays there, left alone.

Her trousers were open, and her shirt stuck to her like a single torn shred.

Five minutes and the calm before the storm would not have changed its meaning forever.
Five minutes and she would have arrived home safely with the feeling of secrecy in her heart.

But no, he had seen her and he had felt a sense of restlessness, he had taken her over feociously like the storm had taken over the sea.

It had not mattered to him, for him, she was only one of the many seas in which he had beaten his waves, but the sea was now restless. It kept moving, throwing huge waves, and had the feeling that it would never again be able to come to rest.

She laid there quite still from the outside, but her thoughts dragged her to the bottom in a vortex beneath the surface of the water.

She laid there for a long time, until the waves subsided, leaving a stillness, a stillness of death.

What had just been marked by loud noises and deafening rumblings, by man-high waves and metre-deep swirls now lays broken, calm and smooth and torn.

Now she also came to know the calm after the storm, and she despaired.

Her thoughts appeared again on the surface of the water, but it was too late, she was dead, her thoughts had drowned.

Yet she lived, laying on the ground as a silent shell, breathing without being alive. The calm after the storm ate her up, for she had nothing familiar, she was nothing, but a cruel emptiness left behind by the storm.

Now she really understood the sea, and from now on she hated the smell of the calm before the storm, for she had felt the suffering that the sea had to undergo.

Were you worth it?

I wish I had taken the train.

I stood at the station of life, and I wish I had gotten on the train. I wish I had left so that I would never have met you.

But I wonder, do I really wish I had never known you?

What kind of person would I be today if I hadn't been broken by you back then?

But I wonder, do I really wish I had never known you?

What kind of person would I be today if I hadn't had to heal myself because of you?

But I wonder, do I really wish I had never known you?

For what would have become of all those moments that made me so overjoyed?

Was my momentary euphoria worth later being so demolished, having to laboriously pick up my soul in a thousand pieces from the stone cold ground?

Yes, I think you were worth it.

You were never really good to me, but in the times when I was unaware of this fact, you were able to make me overjoyed.

Rebellion

Hair holds memories, so I am cutting it all off.

I separate myself from the experiences that destroyed my past and made me crumble in pieces on the cold stone floor.

I extract myself from my past in order to have a future because how is one supposed to keep living after experiencing what I have experienced. There is this deep gap to my heart that if I do not watch out, I will trip and fall into. It is a danger, but it is getting more narrow as the years pass by.

I cut my hair to express myself.
To show who I am, to embody my personality.

I cut my hair as a symbol of growth.

The longer my hair grows back, the stronger I will be.

It is a sign of rebellion. It is like giving my past

the finger for destroying me. It is the determination that I will get better.

At first my motivation to heal was solely out of spite.
To show the people whom I was mistreated by what they have missed out on.

Then I learned the importance of loving myself and my motive became to get better for my own sake, so I cut my hair even shorter.

I did to my hair what needed to be done; I cut it, I coloured it, I styled it. I did to my hair what was done to me, and I let it grow.

I was unable to destroy my hair, and I realized so were the people that tried to with me.

My hair is where I took my strength from to recover, so I decided to give life one more shot and it was to be the best decision that I have ever made.

Thank you to everyone that is currently showing me how much live is worth living. I love you and *I love me!*

16/10/2027

Every day in our lives is different and special in its own way.

There are days that make us happy, and there are days that make us sad. Days that appear rarely are days like the sixteenth of October.

Days like the sixteenth of October are days that throw our lives completely off track, without even thinking about it when we get out of bed in the morning.

Days like the sixteenth of October can be positive, or negative.

Days like the sixteenth of October not only make fundamental changes to our lives and our perspective on events, but days like the sixteenth of October change us as people.
Days like the sixteenth of October creep into our consciousness, then insidiously merge with our personality and become an integral part of it.

Days like the sixteenth of October do not necessarily have to take place on this date, but for me personally, it is the day that comes to mind when I think about a profound change of events.

As I indicated before, I think personality is fluid, we all have this basic set of feelings and emotions, but even these are malleable.

Until we experience a day like the sixteenth of October, we are a lump of clay that is soft and kneadable and, above all, accessible to all.

Now, if we experience a day like the sixteenth of October, we acquire something that not only deforms us, but adds up to us.

We receive something that closes a cage around our clay insides. This cage has a door, but only the door itself decides when and for whom it opens.

Days like the sixteenth of October are experiences that render the basic set of emotions in us unnecessary, as they enter with such presence and abundance that they kill the person we once were.

Days like the sixteenth of October steal our naivety and shape us to such an extent that it would take a far-reaching event like the sixteenth of October to distort us in another direction.

However, do not get me wrong; events like the sixteenth of October do not always need to be grotesque under everyone's eyesight, it is enough that they have a personal meaning.

Nevertheless, I am not convinced that days like the sixteenth of October rob us of our former selves in immutable completeness.

I am under the impression, that days like the sixteenth of October, with their massive force, do not completely erase our personality base, but put us in a bright red, coma-like state.

It is then up to us whether we want to keep what days like the sixteenth of October establish us as our new personality, or whether we want to work determinedly to return to our (true) old selves.

Empty phrases

"But it made you so much stronger"

That is what they always tell you, but the question no one asks is whether it was worth it, whether it was all worth it, just to be stronger in the end.

But what does the end of something like this mean?

Sure, at some point the screaming and crying and despair will become less, but the end?

And sure, at some point the voices in your head will become quieter, and you will come to terms with the fact that it happened, but the end?

The end is a word that you really only hear from unillumined people in this context.
Of course, everything will eventually get better and the wounds will become scars, but they are not gone.

I think the main problem, why outsiders do not understand this, is because they limit the thing to a minimum. They truly and wholeheartedly believe that there once happened something, that is now over and gone. For people that never had to undergo a torture like this it seems like just a normal Friday, when in our reality whole worlds were broken down.

What most people do not seem to understand is that the possibility of a normal development is taken away from us strategically, because we are busy enough to survive and still pretend that we are doing well, because otherwise we get to hear that it was not so bad after all, and we should not over-dramatize the thing.
"It was just..."
"So others must go through..."
"If you experienced... I could understand you, but like this..."

And then there is this constant talk of understanding. No! You do not understand anything! Understanding is only done by those who have had to travel the same path, who were once in our own skin, but otherwise?

No, otherwise understanding is the wrong word.

Perhaps it is given to particularly empathetic people to relate to our feelings or even recreate them up to a certain point, but it is never the case that an outsider can understand.

And for this very reason, when we are asked how we are doing, we smile and nod, and always hide away all of our emotions, which is abysmal for our healing, when we have to suppress everything and accumulate it ourselves.

On the one hand nobody really wants to know how we are doing. It is just a polite question people expect you to answer dishonestly to, because they are already caught up enough in their own lives.

On the other hand we live in constant fear of being judged by outside people for what happened to us, because once again, they do not possibly have the ability to understand.

We are doomed to grow up, instead of being the child we are, because of the massiveness of our situation.

And the best thing is that others always praise you for being so mature for your age, without realizing why.

L is for Love

Elements of love

A breath of air,
slightly brushing through my hair,
your hands,
a part of sky,
wind.

The sand I sit on,
soft and warm,
your lap,
a part of the beach,
earth.

The ocean's browsing,
deep and blue,
your eyes,
a part of the sea.
water.

The feeling in me,
inflaming whenever I think of you,
my heart,
a part of you,
fire.

The fire motive – wooden puppet turn yourself

If you ever are to fall in love with a person, fall
in love with their eyes.

Throughout your lifetime your whole body
changes.
Your hair tuns grey, your weight alternates,
your skin will eventually wrinkle.

The only thing able to always stay young and so
full of the life you fell in love with are one's
eyes.

Eyes are a portal to one's soul.

When we look in the darkness our pupils
widen because they want to take in all the light
in order to properly see.

When we look at a person we love, the exact
same reaction is performed, as we long for tak-
ing in all of the light shining from that person.

Through our eyes, emotions are outspoken,

that could never be communicated in words, as they are too banal to express all the depth of ones most profound feelings.

Through our eyes, words are spoken that never touch our tongue, that never cross the border of our lips.

Our eyes silently communicate, what our mouth is too afraid to tell.

When I look into your eyes, my pupils always widen and I try to place all of my love, all of my deepest emotions in my gaze, whishing you would understand the signs, because I am unable to tell you in any other way.

An evening at the beach

Looking in the fire,
thinking about you.

My heart enflamed,
like wood and grass.

My heart is owned by you!

A letter

A letter, a little piece of infinity in your hand.

I will never stop writing about you.

I will write to you and about you and I will dedicate to you with my words infinity.

I will make you immortal.

You do not deserve just a paragraph or two, you deserve whole novels written about the beauty of your soul.

I will write you letters,
forever,
because in twenty years you will not find messenger messages in a box in your attic and smile.

Do you still think, or do you already feel?

A girl,
so beautiful,
so magical,
angelic.

With her grace she casts me under her spell,
I am wax between her fingers.

What no one else can see,
She never leaves my head.

Love once was heavy,
hard to hold,
with her as simple as to float.

With her I fall on clouds,
through her I grew my wings.

Cursed

Your presence has the ability to take away my breath.

Whenever you enter a room, I am always star-struck.

I am amazed by your natural charms, and it is a secret to me how one can be so amazingly beautiful inside and out.

My heart is stumbling over the deepest feelings I hold for you and will be unable to let go of forever.

Or to say it in shorter words:
I love you!

eloquent

Do I understand that right?

The biggest lie I tell myself is that I understand, because I understand nothing.

I understand, that I do not, but at the same time I do not understand, as I think to understand, that I do not understand, in which I claim myself an understanding which I still do not have.

I believe I understand, but everything I do know is just a blurry and unimportant mess in the ruling of the universe.

What I know, what I think to know can be true, or it can be false, it is not to change anything.
What I know, what I think to know can be true at this very moment, but false in the next.

I believe I know nothing, but what do I know?
Maybe I also know everything.
I don't know (or do I)...

Optimistic philanthropy, but...

Child! Enjoy your youth! These are the years of
your life. I really can't understand what your
generation is always fantasising with problems.
We used to, we had war, we had problems, but
you... Be grateful!

The youth of today... so spoiled, so sensitive, so
softened.
Problems... oh as if they knew something about
problems.
Live children, live finally, there is nothing that
worries you.

Yes, yes... already understood.
Optimistic philanthropy and we bleatingly lay
on a sunlit flower meadow, instead of rampag-
ing around on it and being happy with our
lives.

A world full of possibilities that we do not use,
we arrogant pessimistic youth.

A world of possibilities that we do not use

because we unable to thus the sun is shining.
The sun is blood red.

Yes, yes, I should enjoy my carefree youth, optimistic philanthropy, but Ukraine is being bombed.

Sure, grateful that everyone is doing well these days, optimistic philanthropy, but the children in the Yemen area are starving.

Of course, everyone is living in peace, optimistic philanthropy, but in Gaza people are being shot.

A happy childhood, optimistic philanthropy, but in Palestine children are becoming soldiers.

True, there is enough of everything for everyone, totally just now, optimistic philanthropy, but in Israel people have nothing to eat.
Everyone is fine, because the sun is shining, but the sun is shining blood red, because the world is in ruins, crumbles and bits.
War, climate crisis, a school systems about to

crash, people without humanity and people who work sixteen hours a day but still are unable to afford bread.

Rich people who are getting richer. A red carpet for the Hunger Games.

One planet, but Two Worlds.

A flower meadow full of sunshine, but the sun is shining blood red, because the world is in ruins, crumbles and bits, because of a society that isn't one, a society in strife.

Racism, classism, sexism, war and violence; we really have worse problems than a man who puts on makeup, two women who love each other, or a human who is just a person.

Optimistic philanthropy, I am a friend of positive thinking, optimistic philanthropy, but positive thinking would really not be philanthropic in this case.

Now I stand here in a world where the sun

drips from the sky in blood-red rays, grins mockingly at our crumbling world and casts its violent shadows upon us.

I stand here in this world and would love to do good, but I don't even know where to start. Everything I can do seems so miserably small.

I stand here in this world and would love to do good, but I'm overwhelmed by the sheer weight of reality.

I stand here in this world and would love to do good, but it's almost impossible to keep up with each and every one of our world's problems. The amount of information that hits you in one day takes three to process.

I stand here, in a world steeped in the blood-red light of the sun that derides our humanity.

I stand here, looking at our society and I am unable to blame the sun.

We rather hate than love, we hate love, but we

also hate hate, and especially we hate the hate over love.

Self-help group Humanity, cheers!

We are a paradox, incomprehensible, incomplete.

I am simply unable to understand how we are so addicted to drama but complain that there is hardly anything positive to hear on the news. I absolutely cannot understand why we would rather argue than tolerate each other.

Why are superficial things like the colour of our skin, religion, sexuality, gender or social status our yardstick to differentiate between people?

We determine sympathy by superficial characteristics, but what am I really complaining about?

The sun shines, doesn't it?
The sun shines over the flower meadow of our

society, where the biggest plants are problems but the blades of grass are outnumbered.

The blades of grass are so many, and if they wait for the wind to sway them all in the same direction, then they could manage to trump the big plants.

One day the sun will shine yellow again, instead of blood red, because one day we will all be smart enough to work together, to see the common good and not just our own, we will join hands instead of pulling all on different threads in opposite directions. If you turn two gears in an engine against each other, their teeth break off.

Everything would have been able to function, only the stubbornness ruins the system.

I am laying here, on the flower meadow staring at the drops of the blood-red sun.

I look around and I notice that everyone

around me seems to be wearing sunglasses. For them the sun looks yellow.

In a tunnel vision, they stare at the yellow sun without noticing the shadows of the large plants even on the edge.

Yes, I think, it may take a while until the sun is yellow again.

A thought bubbles up inside of me and before I can really grasp it, I scream loudly "blood-red".

The people around me stare at me, torn out of their trance by the noise. They take off their sunglasses to see me. They are blinded by the blood-red glow of the sun. Some stay upright, next to me and now also see the shadows of the grotesque plants, but most are unable to stand the sight of the blood-red sun.

They put their sunglasses back on their faces and continue to stare in a trance-like tunnel view into the sky.
Yes, I think to myself. At some point it will be

time for all of us to take off our sunglasses and
then, only then, the hour of change has struck.

The blindness of being able to see

Which society do we live in?

This is now a question that is often asked,
where does society begin, where does society
end?

Do we live in one or are we many?
Many, broken pieces of what was once one.
But was it?
Was it one?
Are we one?
Or are we many?
Many individuals who taunt where they can,
who do not fit together like pieces of a thou-
sand different puzzles.

We are different and tear each other to shreds
in pursuit of power, for even more power.

Power is our never-ending addiction, everyone
wants it and only the strongest can have it, but
yet we do not understand that there is much
more that unites us than divides us.

We run so fast on the way up that we barely notice the beautiful landscape at the side of the road.

We look for the weaknesses of others instead of their strengths, look for differences instead of equations, look for distance instead of cohesion. But one thing we have not understood; actually we are all the same, we are all one society, because we are all human.

We are all human beings who all have their individual beauty. It is time to build bridges and let go of how we look, where we come from, who we love, what progenitor we believe in or what gender we are.

It is often said that we need to open our eyes to become a better society, but wouldn't it actually be better if we closed our eyes?

Wouldn't we actually see more if we were blind?

Because then we would not even have the

chance to judge other people based on factors outside of their personality.
If we were blind, in my opinion, we would all be closer, because only we would count as humans.

I believe that at the moment we are many small societies, many small islands in the middle of a large sea.

Like-minded people who surround themselves with other like-minded people.
But what like-minded people are, we are usually not so sure, because the more controversial our opinion is, the harder we find it to justify it, even if we are not so wrong after all.

Just for fear of being banished to our own little island, away from our society, away from our so-called like-minded people we fall silent.
Often we also tend to double standards, others have done that, how Terrible?
But so do I?
Ah, half as bad.
We are not open enough, which actually only

breaks us down, because the less open we are, the less we accept other people, the more wonderful personalities and perspectives remain hidden from us.

I do not intend to say that, to live in a good society, we all have to be best friends, rather the opposite, our world revolves through discussion, but at the end of the day it must be clear that we can only become a society if we are able to live with other people having different opinions.

And by that I mean opinion, not the self-granted privilege of restricting the lives of others. An opinion is what concerns you.
An opinion is to say what you want, for yourself, what you don't want for yourself, or what you can't imagine, for yourself.

A self-granted privilege to restrict the lives of others is to say what you do not want others to do with their own lives.

I have no intentions of glorifying behaviours

like racism, classism, sexism, discrimination, homophobia or, in shorter terms, cognitive dysfunction, because they are not opinions. They are the self-granted privilege of restricting the lives of others.

What I mean by my words is, that we should not only accept the opinions of everyone but must do so in order to live in a society.

Butterfly Effect

Everything we say and do matters!

No matter how lapidary it may seem to us, our words and actions can influence people for better or worse.

We never know what's going on in other people, we don't know their perspective or history, and yet we measure ourselves to judge.

We form an opinion about a scene we are unable to see all of because half of the curtains are down.

Many people would say we kill others without picking up a weapon, but I would like to correct this mistake, we kill not without a weapon, but even with the most powerful one that humanity has.

We constantly underestimate it, we do not know how to use it, yet it is our greatest power, the power of our words.

It is an immeasurable power from which comes an even greater responsibility.

But this responsibility is not accepted by most people, not out of prudence but out of a lack of knowledge.

Often, we fail to realise that a sentence, even a single word, can cause more grotesque damage than the button on a nuclear device.

Language is a playground for the rich

She who is rich is given a brain.

She who scolds herself rich because she bathes
in money, she has not understood life.

She who appreciates what she has without rest-
ing on it, she who is unable to underestimate
the power of language and is aware that lan-
guage is a playground for the rich has under-
stood the value of life.

Language gives us power, and we give language
power.

She who is rich knows better than to judge
those who have less.

She who is rich may on the contrary not judge
at all, because this leads to immediate homoge-
nization in the tough pulp of humanity and the
privilege of standing out is no longer to be
called her own.

She who is rich sees being different not as a burden but as an opportunity, not to get more power, but to improve the world a little every day.

For if we open our eyes a little bit wider, we see in clear outlines that if everyone has power, we all have more power.

Substance

The more we find out, the sooner we realize
how little we know.

A found answer raises five new questions, if
that is enough.
So, if we as humans want to know as much as
possible in order to create clarity, we can ask
ourselves the question whether it is good for us
to try to know everything, or whether by the
failed attempt of finding the way we realize that
we are actually long past our goal, and have
paved the way in vain, without a goal.

We sting in the dark in search of the needle in
the haystack, without realizing that it has al-
ready been placed on a red velvet pillow next to
it.

Knowledge is beyond question helpful for hu-
mans, but the question arises, how much of it
is good for us?

Humans have the strange peculiarity of

classifying everything into doses; how many tablets on which body, how much contact until it is considered rude, how much millilitres of oat milk to make the cake taste good. We humans simply categorize, catalogue and dose everything, everything, except our knowledge.

Because, as we know, you can never have enough knowledge, I mean, it is clear, because otherwise, we would never put children's health at risk through a completely overloaded school system.

Otherwise knowledge would not regulate know how much money we earn, and thus how our lives go.

Or shorter, knowledge is power and trough our constant addiction to power we aim for as much knowledge as possible.

Why don't we start by asking ourselves if knowledge is really that good, considering that the most educated and intellectual among us are those who also have the most anxiety states.

We see knowledge as progress and as something good, and I don't want to deny that, actually I do agree, but I do also believe we should try to find an answer to the question of how much knowledge is good for us?

Thought thoughtless thoughts

We were told to think.

So We thought.
Or so we thought.
Until we found out that our thinking was impaired.

We thought about thinking, and we thought about what the people who obviously do not think are thinking.

We thought about whether thinking was a compromise or an essential process of the brain.

We thought we should try not to think, but that failed, because we thought about what it felt like not to think, and those were thoughts again.

So we decided that one could not not think, but then we looked at the world, at our world.

We thought, how could this happen if one had

to think, because the world looked like a tangle of structures that definitely could not have been created by thinking.
We thought.
We thought that thinking was a concept that could not be interrupted, but it was not the same for everyone.

We thought that some people only think so far that it is smart to go after leaders, and we thought we should ask ourselves if we can declare this thinking to be thinking.

We thought that maybe there is a thinking that is easier for people who are not up to thinking about thinking. A kind of inclusive program. A kind of sub-thinking.

We thought that if there was this sub-thinking, how about just doing what a thinking thinker says, and we tried to think that we wanted to stop thinking.
We tried to narrow our horizons to the state of sub-thinking.

We thought that we had succeeded, but then we noticed.

In the end, we had only thought of thinking because they told us to think, so we only thought we were thinking.
 However we thought that we were thinking because we had noticed that we had only been thinking because we had been told to think.
We thought that we should ask ourselves the question of whether we were thinkers or not.

We thought that asking ourselves that question would be a good idea to find out if we were thinking.

We thought that we were thinking only because someone had told us to think, but we were thinking about thinking, and we were thinking without having heard the thoughts of others.

We thought we were on a good track, until we found that we were all so confused by thinking about thinking that thinking and thinking about thinking seemed almost impossible.

And then we thought one last thought that made us realize that there is a difference between sub-thinking and thinking together, and that one thought for oneself, even if one thought together.

We understood that in order to understand thinking, we had to think together, because thinking alone was impossible, because there was not only thinking and sub-thinking. We understood that everyone thought that everyone thought the same thing and therefore thought the way one thought themselves.

We understood that it was important to think together to understand thinking, because no one could think properly about thinking alone.

We also understood that there was not only one right way of thinking, but that the following principle had to apply; to think and to let think.

We understood that thought thoughts about thinking could only be right if they did not restrict anyone else in their thinking.

We understood that any thinking that allowed all thinking to happen, was good, as long as one thought and did not leave the thinking to thinking thinkers. For anyone who thinks that it is a well-thought-out idea to leave the thinking to other thinking thinkers should think again instead of thinking what others think and leaving the real thinking to thinking thinkers, for that is not thinking.

In the end, we thought we had understood thinking.

However, we soon realized that this could not be the truth, because thinking about thinking is an endlessly complex cycle, and we thought that was perfectly fine, because if one always gains direct clarity through thinking, it would be unnecessary to think, since the process of thinking would finally be finite.

That would make thinking easier, but we were thinking right in thinking that thinking was not meant to be easy.

The complexity of being complex

Our dear mind is a strange thing.

It is so complicated in its structure with all
those feelings and facts and confusion but at
the same time it is so easy to manipulate.

There are people going crazy over a simple
word, committing crimes and murder over it,
while it is just a word, not a real thing.

Our mind is a master at connecting events to
patterns while leaving out of regard that confus-
ing possibility with probability is quite a dan-
gerous thing, because it can easily make you
lose your mind.

As our brain might be so complicated, that
even world scientists fail to fully understand its
function, it is so simple, that our subconscious-
ness is able to elevate and twist, what our con-
sciousness thinks is real for a fact.

A curse worth envying

Pretty stones

She swam in the sea of diamonds but still she drowned.

She had everything, but still she drowned.

She swam in the sea of diamonds, but while trying to swim she cut her skin on the sharp edges of the stones.

She swam in the sea of diamonds and everyone admired her as they saw the shine and sparkle, everyone admired her as they saw the smile on her lips, but they did not see her eyes, her eyes, her iris swallowed by pain.

She swam in the sea of diamonds and everybody saw that she had everything.

She swam in the sea of diamonds, and everybody was jealous of her because they did not see that under the surface, the diamonds turned into rubies coloured by the blood of her *wounds.*

Trapped in between two worlds

I am a human being.

I am a human being with a body and a soul.

I am stuck between two worlds.

My body, it holds me in this reality, in the reality of life around me, in the reality where time is measured in years I spent in this world.

However, my soul rebels deafeningly loud.

I am a human being with a body and a soul.

I am a human being whose body has to grow into the reality of its soul's being.

I know who I am, I already knew before they told me.

Before they told me, it was almost more obvious to me than from the moment they tried to break me down, my personality, into scientific

units. I am a genius, they said, with their clip-
boards and white coats, but I find that to be
highly arrogant.

Folding me as a person up in such a manner,
buckling up, stomping me down to one word...
genius. I want to laugh so bad I want to cry.

I am a human being!

I am a human being, who could not care less
about these scientific measurements. I am a hu-
man being, that has no advantages from this
knowledge.
In a world where only numbers count, in our
world where the pressure to perform and the
compulsion to compare prevails, it helps me
there, yes... but with what counts?

The qualities I look for in people are way ahead
of just numbers. Good people are not defined
by intelligence, or for a fact, not by any other
scientific measurement.

Good people, people worth admiring are those

who are empathetic, those who treat others
with love and respect, those who stand up for
others and show social courage.

Those good qualities, those important qualities,
you find among everyone, no matter their intel-
ligence, no matter their race, no matter their
gender, no matter their age.

I have always looked for friends my age, both
my ages. I am a person who is happy because
she can adapt and feel home in so many groups
of people.

I am a human being, not a number or even a
word.

I am me, and I am valuable, and sometimes I
forget that.

To be seen metaphorically

Stolen Wealth

I listen to him talk.

He talks and talks and will not stop. He goes on, he proceeds, he does not even take a breath.

He keeps on whining about his stolen wealth. He was rich once, but then he lost all of his money on that stupid bet.

From that day on, he kept on going to this bar, to my bar.

Every day he orders a negroni and whines about how terrible his life is, now that he has lost everything.
Every day I serve him a negroni and I listen to him whining.

He talks about his wife and his kids and how much the love him, and he whines about how terrible his life is, because he has lost everything, every penny of his.

Every day when I serve him a negroni, I see messages and missed calls pop up on his phone. One says "Honey, I am really looking forward to you coming home later!" another "Good night dad, I love you!"

He looks at those messages and sometimes he replies.

After he puts his phone down, he keeps on whining about the fact that he does not have anything left.
All of his money, gone.

He whines about how the bank took all of his most important belongings, everything of worth to him, while in the background his wedding song is playing.

I do my job, I serve him a negroni and I listen to him whining.

I tell him that I feel sorry for him and he screams at me that I could never understand what he has to go through every day.

All his wealth...stolen.

I nod at him and tell him that he is right, that I have no idea how terrible this must feel.

I look at the clock. It is midnight, twelve o'clock.

My shift is over so I clock out and go home.

I lay down on my mattress in my lonely one-bedroom apartment and I think;

No, I really do not have a clue of what stolen wealth could feel like.

Roses have thorns

Once upon a time roses were the most inno-
cent creatures, full of dignity and beauty.

People saw her outshining presence and tried
to have her for themselves.

People killed the rose out of selfishness and
took their corpses home, expecting them to be
magnificent forever.

Corpses rot, and after a week the rose lost her
last dignity being thrown into the garbage.

Once upon a time roses were the most inno-
cent creatures full of dignity and beauty, but
and then they were touched so they grew
thorns.

They grew thorns so that everybody who tried
to hurt them would only add on to her blood-
red beauty.

The roses beauty lays within being untouched, so her thorns are coloured in the same shade as her petals, drenched by the blood of the people that tried to end her.

I don't know (TW: Mention of death, suicide, abuse)

They asked: „What is the saddest word in your opinion?"
"Grief"
"being afraid"
"Death"
"being petrified"
"Hatred"
"maybe and just", was my answer.
"And why is that?", they asked me with confusion in their eyes.

That was, when I remembered the time, they told me "You are great and smart and stuff, but you are just not enough for me"

The time where all I wanted to do was scream "I am just a child, leave me alone" came to my mind.

I caught a glimpse at the second where they told me "It was just seconds that killed him. Maybe if there haven't been so many people who wanted to watch in our way, we could have saved him"

"I am sorry, maybe you are just better off without me", were the last words I spoke to her.

"I just cannot take it anymore", was the last thing they texted me before they jumped.

I remembered me thinking "Maybe I am just not enough"

"I don't know", I replied.

Colouring the sky (TW: Mention of suicide, scars)

We sit in a meadow and look at the sunset.

You tell me the story of how angels colour the sky every night, with brushes, laboriously.

I smile... how much I enjoy the time I spend with you, and yet I do not appreciate it in the way I would have if only I had known...

We sit there for a long time, talking, and at some point the stars appear above our heads.

We look up, enjoy their sight. I tell you that each of them is a loved one waving at us from the sky.

You smile at me and tell me that one day you will wave at me the brightest. I do not understand what you are actually telling me with these words. I do not understand that they were not just sweetly said flakes, but a serious prophecy.

It is beyond me that one day might not be in sixty years, but soon, too soon.

We talk, and talk, and you tell me how glad you are to have me.
We fall asleep together, on a blanket under stars, and when I wake up the next morning, you are gone, because you are no longer there.

I find out over a phone-call, and as your mother's soft voice trembles through the speaker of my phone, I break down.

At your funeral, I hug you one last time, and I feel the cuts on your wrists, wounds that never had the chance to become scars.

I sit in the meadow, our meadow, watching the sunset.

I think of you and your wounds.
You are an angel, have never been anything else.
An angel on earth who could not bear the pain and suffering of the world because his soul, due

to its nature, was too pure, too kind-hearted, too vulnerable.
The sunset is so much more beautiful since you are no longer with me, because you paint so much better than all the other angels!

When the night falls and the stars rise, I see one shining brightly, and I know that is you! I sit there and see your face smiling in the stars.

I feel my eyes fill with tears, because even though I know that you are better now, that you are at home, that you are happy, my angel, yet my soul aches that I will never be able to hear your voice again, that I will never be able to feel your embrace again.

For [...], I love you so infinitely much little one, and I would have never forgiven myself if you could not have read this text.

Survival and Death (TW: Graphic details of a happening suicide)

She sits there, and no one really notices her.

When people look at her, they only see a woman, a young woman with a smile on her lips, always trying to be kind to everyone.

What no one notices are the dark garlands under her eyes, because she laughs. What no one sees is the rest of mascara in the corner of her eye, which she forgot to wipe away when she tried to hide that she was crying.
Not that she had to, no one cared anyway, but she cared a lot about maintaining the facade, right up to the bittersweet end.

She raises her hand.
Yes?
May I please use the bathroom?
Sure.

She gets up and leaves the room.

In her hand her bag, *some wonder, no one asks.*

She enters the washroom, closes the door behind her, but she does not need to lock it, because no one cares about her anyway.

She wants to do it today.

She can't stand it any longer.
She has persevered for so long, so long.
She has obtained from doing it, so she doesn't hurt her family, her friends, her family who insults and despises her, and her friends who cheat her.

She takes out her phone, opens her tracker.

A blue icon with the words "Clean for 461 days" lights up.

She scrolled down.

"Your reasons" is depicted now.

Below is a colourful pile of pictures and a few written lines.
She looks at the reasons one by one.

Her friends? Wrong. Delete.
Her family? Humiliating. Delete.
Her favorite food? Irrelevant. Delete.
So she goes on and eventually there's only one reason left, her.

"Because I want to live and not just survive, and I want to love and I want to be loved," the quote says said.

How naive she had been then.
She would never really be loved by anyone, she knew now, and she also knew that she didn't want to love, because to love without being loved back was even more painful than not loving at all. Bullshit. Delete.

Now there was nothing standing beneath the "Your reasons" banner. And that was right. She had no reason to stay.

Her eyes filled with tears, she knew all along that there was nothing left that was valuable to her in this life, but to see it that way broke the last tiny piece of heart, what had been whole.

She was now in a state of complete disarray.

She put a chair under the doorknob, just to be sure she would not be disturbed.
She opens her bag, pulls out the pack.

She closes the bag and puts it in a corner.
She looks into the mirror "Emo" she hears in her ears.
Pill one.
"Go cut yourself" "You're not important to us anyway"
Pill two.
"Can't you ever be normal"
"Stop and just be like your sister, it can't be that hard"
Pill three and four.
She gets hot.
"You're a single disappointment"
Pill five.

Slowly you start to get sick. The double vision starts to chime in. She holds on to the sink. The cool porcelain on her glowing skin keeps her in this shattering reality.
She needs to move faster.

Pill six.
His eerily disgusting laughter stops in her ears again.
Pill seven and eight.
She loses her footing. Her legs give way and she lands on the floor in a strangely twisted, crippled position.
Her exterior shows her inner life.

She must swallow at least one more time. A tentative knock on the door breaks the silence.

Pill nine.
The knocking gets louder, becomes a shaking.
Pill ten.

She hears a voice screaming, thinks distorted to hear her name.
Pill eleven.

The last thing she hears is the door fly open,
and someone screaming "call an ambul…"

Then everything is black.
Black, nothing but black.
She made it.
She's dead.
White.
Is she in heaven?
But why is it beeping sound in heaven.
A chair in the corner and a bed in which she
sits in materialize.
There is something on the chair.
Something that is now rushing towards her.
Then she looks into those beautiful sky-blue
eyes that she loves so much, but something is
strange because today the skin around them is
red and swollen.

She has survived, and yet a tiny little star has
just appeared in the midst of her darkness, and
she has the feeling that she might be able to live
after all, and until then she decides to survive.

Arrogant

She is happy, so damn happy.

She dances to the music, she laughs, she has fun. She has not felt like this for a very long time, so free, so uninhibited.

'You're so arrogant,' he says, because she's good. She's scored a hit, she's happy about her hit. Not overly so, but her smile had widened a little.

They have known each other for a short time, but they are far from being strangers.

She feels a pang in the pit of her stomach. 'You really think I'm arrogant?' she asks in a tone that implies that now is the right time to tell the truth.
She knows that he does not think she is arrogant, no, actually she does not, but she hopes he doesn't.

'Yes, actually, I do,' he replies, and she feels the twinge in her stomach grow stronger.

There is nothing worse for her than this one insult.

She has heard it all before, and she has never cared. She is a woman and she is successful. Of course, being called names is her daily fate, but that one word triggered feelings in her that came close to the force of an immense dam breaking. This one person, this damn one person, always called her arrogant when she was angry with her, and it hurt.

Arrogant hurt.

She sat down.
Her smile had disappeared, but no one noticed.

She sat there, noticed her damn eyes filling with damn tears, and wanted her eyes to stay dry so that no one would notice how "arrogant" affected her.

It was her turn again.
She thought only one thought, which in that moment was enough to fill her entire brain.

Do not score, do not score, just do not damn score. She scored. She was not happy. She was frustrated. She was hurt.

She had not wanted to score, had not wanted to be arrogant, but at least she had not been happy this time.
Maybe that made it tolerable for him.
He came up to her, they had known each other for a long time.
He had heard everything. He asked, "Why aren't you happy?" She looked at him, she looked at him trying her best to not cry, she said, "I better not be too happy"
"But joy has nothing to do with arrogance!"

She flees.
To the bathroom.
She is alone.

Tears fill her eyes again.
When she looks in the mirror above the sink, she does not see herself.
She sees arrogance. She breaks.
She knows how she is.

She is smart.
She is good at school, but actually she always
makes an effort to sweep it all under the carpet.

She knows that it is not the things in life that
matter.
If someone asked her what she values, it would
never be these qualities, also these qualities, but
not primarily these qualities.

Much more would be empathy, openness and
the ability not to judge people. She tries to em-
body these qualities and usually succeeds, but it
is the case that most people simply do not care,
because she is successful, and people do not like
to see that. That is why she is used to being in-
sulted, but arrogant, arrogant hurts.

She goes back.
Sits down,
silent.
She's a wreck, she has to pull herself together
so that the water doesn't run out of her eyes
like a tsunami.

She does what she always does when she needs to calm down.

She calls her blue eyes in front of her inner vision. Her beautiful, sea-blue eyes, which usually have the same energetic spark as her eyes.

She hears her reassuringly soft voice in her ears. Listens as she says, "You need to focus," pointing to her eyes.

"You need to breathe, breathe with me. Deep, and deep again."

She feels her left hand, the place where her hand had briefly lingered on hers, taking away her sense of restlessness and replacing it with that of security.

Words, many of them, my heart, my soul

Antithetically

You cannot speak in poetry to someone who
does not read.

You cannot force a stone to not be hard.

You cannot force feelings out of a place where
there are none.

You cannot constantly put faith into somebody
that keeps on disappointing you.

You cannot moan grass while expecting it not
to be shorter in the end.

You cannot pick a flower and expect it not to
die of thirst.

You cannot hold a lighter and hold it next to
wood while expecting it not to burn.

You cannot to one thing and expect the oppo-
site to happen.

You cannot expect things to happen whilst ignoring all the signs.

Words

My words are my home.

When I write, I am at home.

I am my words, and my words are me.

Trough them I express myself, through them I am.
If I did not have words, I would not have thoughts. If I did not have words, I would not be able to articulate myself.

Words give me the opportunity to not only be me, but also to live out me.

Words are my home, because they are where I can escape when my world collapses and the chimneys on the endless rooftops of the city start to look like tombstones in a cemetery again.

In general, I think that cemeteries are the richest places on our planet, because there are so many words buried beside people.

Words that were never spoken,
words that were shouted out into the world,
words that would have better been said,
words, about feelings,
words, about love, hate, jealousy, longing, passion and friendship.
Words, about ideas,
words that only would have had to be spoken out to completely change the course of things, to tear the world apart and make it turn in a different direction.

But sometimes, sometimes my words also fail me.

When I try to rewrite the level of perfection that you, my beloved, embody, I fail bitterly every time.

Every word seems too lapidary, too ordinary...

But I wonder; is this because of the imperfection of the words themselves, or because of my inability to use them properly?
Am I trying too desperately to express something with words that only the heart can describe?

Do words have limits?

I think so, because even the most well-sounding, perfect, beautiful, eloquent, nonchalant word that the world has ever heard is, in its power to imprint, seen individually by every beholder, and thus unable to reflect all-embracing perfection.

Words are good for gaining clarity, words are good for communicating.

But words are simply not capable of expressing what is so individual that it cannot simply be communicated. Emotions.

We all feel emotions in different ways.
Our feelings are not only situationally

individual, but also feel different in themselves
for each person.
Emotions in their purest, most profound form
are probably what even words fail at.

From me for you

A letter from me for you, to show you my deepest feelings.

With a letter from me to you, I give you my words and with them a piece of my own heart.

With a letter from me to you, you get a piece of me for you.

I am my words, my words are me.

They are my medium to express myself, to reveal my personality to the world.
My words are my heart and my words are my way of warmly hugging people with my heart.

My words are special, the most special thing about me, about everyone.

We can all speak, yet it is also our language that makes us individual.

We all speak differently, and while some destroy with their words, others manage to build things up with their words, open new lives and create peace.

My words are a special part of mine, not only because I understood the power of language, but also because I can use them to express my love for you.

Writing for me is like exhaling.

It is emptying the soul and feeling in control.

It is a piece of self-created freedom, it is from me for you.

Of what I left behind

Everything is great!

She laughs,
she sings,
she dances.

Everything is great!

She is the most optimistic person,
the most kind,
the most hurt.

She cries,
she begs,
she screams in pain.

Everything is great!

She is the most optimistic person,
because she wants people to see the good,
the most kind,
because she wants people to see their worth,
the most hurt,
because nobody notices her crumbling.

Parched

Those who lack of love will get the most creative finding it.

If one is constantly denied love, they will find the most creative ways of feeling loved.

To the thirsty, vinegar looks like water.

A lost boy whose soul is held by nobody's hands gets attached to the one even looking at it.

A lost boy whose heart is held by nobody's hands finds the most similar to it and worships copper like gold.

Someone has never been shown love or affection gets attached way too quickly to the people that show them even the slightest bit of care.

A deer dying of thirst will see the water running through the veins of the trees and will hydrate itself by eating the leaves, overseeing the streaming river just a few steps further.

Do I love you?

Do I love you, or the perfect illusion of you
that my head has created for me?

In my thoughts you are always so infinitely
charming, so incredibly caring, so impossibly
perfect.
You are everything I have ever dreamed of, be-
cause you too are merely the image of my imag-
ination.

It is the you that I want to see because I love
you, or maybe not you, but what my thoughts
have made of you; the flower-bringing gentle-
man, the philosophical charmer.

It is the you that acts as I long for it.
It is the you whose activities reflect the same
profound feelings that I carry for you in my
heart.

At first, I found you attractive, not even your
appearance, but rather the fact that you were
giving me the kind of attention I wanted, and

because I needed someone to apply my hope-
lessly romantic delusions on.

I needed a face for the custom-build personality
my head had already carefully designed for you.

I fell in love with you because you were caring,
charming, and romantic, and yet you were re-
ally just my head, and yet you were really just
who I wanted you to be.

In the world of my thoughts, you wrote me let-
ters and looked me in the eye with the most in-
nocent love.
In reality, you wrote me text messages that
never went beyond two lines, and in your eyes
there was not love but desire to recognize when
you looked at mine, at me, at my body.

I did not love you, but my imagination, the per-
son who was created for me by my head.

I dreamed of someone who knew me inside
and out, but in reality you did not even know
about the green in my eyes.

One is usually unable to really catch a glimpse of it unless I am standing in the sun, or if one looks me in the eye closely, because my eyes are fairly dark.

But how could you know this if you only met me at night, and it was never my eyes that were worthy of your gaze.

In my imagination you were a poet, in my fantasy you were a romantic, someone who professed his love to me by candlelight, and held their head in the stars with me over a glass of red wine.

I wanted to be loved, that was all I wanted, but just as you were the face of my desires, I became the object of your fantasies.

I was so obsessed with the fear of being alone that I tried to compulsively project everything my heart so profoundly longed for anto you as a person.

I did purposefully unsee your true self, because

I could not bear the pain of being alone again, I could not stand the thought, that you were not to be the person I thought I was.

And you? You shamelessly used my naivety for your pleasure. You gave me hopes, and played with my heart, supported by the image that my head produced of you. You took away moments that should have been special.
I painted you as perfect, and you used that to abuse me.

You used me for your own well-being, regardless of my losses.

I had no experience, how could I have had, young, stupid me.
I was probably older than you, but physically I was inferior to you, you had experiences that I could not have called my own at the time.

You were aware, you did n fact not care.

What you did is presumptuous, antisocial, in some ways abusive and therefore unforgivable.

You caused me so much pain, and because of you I was so unhappy.

Partly that may have been because I focused on my delusions of a picture perfect you, seeing you as a person you never were.

On the other hand, it was your fault because you saw how fledgling I was.

You saw that I was not really able to comprehend that I was really object of affection in the end.

You saw that I just wanted to be loved, you even knew my story in the roughest terms, and all you saw in me was the chance to take advantage of me.

Prism of fairness

Flashlights in my eyes,
even brighter than usual,
because water breaks light.

The tears in my eyes,
a prism to fairness,
now not only my soul hurts,
now also my eyes ache.

Dreams A portal to one soul

I am afraid of the darkness.

Actually, it is not the dark, but the night.
I am not petrified of the sun embedding itself
as a shadow between the mountain peaks.

I am afraid of the monsters that only appear
when it gets dark.
I am afraid of the monsters that crawl out from
under my bed when I lay in it.

I am afraid of the monsters that find their way
out of my head into reality when it gets dark.

I am afraid of the monsters that find their way
out of my brain into my consciousness as soon
as I close my eyes.

During the day I have got everything under
control, during the day I am fine, but when
night falls and my limbs groan with exhaustion,
then I am afraid, because then the monsters
come out.

They are the monsters whose corpses I thought I had defeated permanently.

They are not actually monsters, not blood-curdling figures with several rows of fangs and an arm-like skin, actually they are shadows.

Small shadow creatures, which are easily underestimated due to their inconspicuousness.

They are small shadow creatures, from whose mouths an eerie rumbling chimes, which has the power to scare all good into the undergrowth of reality.

They are shadows of my past, which lie painfully over me.

During the day I have my thoughts under control, during the day I have myself under control, during the day I can isolate myself with a clear awareness of what happened once, but at night...

At night the monsters appear, the shadows that

haunt me, while I lie on the mattress where my memories come alive.

In this bed everything seems so real and so little long gone, because here the monsters have nested in my mattress...disgusting little beasts.

During the day I am happy and optimistic, during the day I am among people with whom I feel comfortable and who give me their love.

But at night... at night the monsters come out and they do not let me sleep.

At night I toss and turn from one side to the other and yet find no rest, because the voices of my monsters, my shadows are too rumbling, too scary, too nerve-wracking.

Constant fatiguing is probably the price you pay if you do not manage, are too weak to keep your monsters under control constantly, every day, every minute and every second.

During the day they live in their cage of gold,

shaking the metal rods. The noise is annoying, but bearable.

At night, at night they manage to blow up the diamond lock on their cage door every time.

Then I am exposed, helpless, because they are outnumbered.

In my dream I catch my monsters again. It is bloody and frightening, sometimes disturbing, but the next morning everything is the same.

Everything seems as if nothing has happened.

There is no trace of my nightly fights, because the pools of blood are in my soul, right next to the cage of gold where my monsters now sleep, taking the opportunity to rest for our next fight... how much I envy them.

———
One day the monsters will no longer live in a cage made of gold, but in a cage made of junk. The lock on their door will no longer be made

of diamond but plastic, and from that day on, from that second on, they will not be able to escape any longer.

Acknowledgements

Thank you to everyone who has stood by my side.
Thank you for every encouraging word, every hug, every act of kindness I received.
Thank you to my long-term and short-term acquaintances.
I thank those who know that I like them and those who perhaps don't.

I especially thank the people who were closely involved in the process of writing this book.

Thank you to my wonderful editor Isabell, who can turn the worst into a good thing, and who always manages to make the sun shine in my head, thank you to Julia and Lena, who have commented on almost every one of my group messages, you two are the sweetest people I know, thank you to Juliette, who rarely says anything, but always finds the moment when I need her words the most, you don't know it but sometimes you are my rock, thanks to Alicia, to whom I owe some titles of my works and who always makes me laugh with her direct way of commenting on things, thanks to Theresa, who always has my back, and who shares my passion for writing, thanks to all of you, because you are always there for me and (mostly) don't make me feel like a burden. You people deserve the world, so I will give you mine! (Consensually) feel hugged by me! <33

I would also like to thank L, who is not the main character in this work, but still manages to motivate me and who keeps me going, even when I don't really feel like it. The best thing is, dear L, you have no idea who you are, that you are L, and no idea that you are motivating me. Dramatic irony... (I will probably tell you one day, if I ever see the slightest chance of not being rejected :))

I would also like to thank a person whose name I am unable mention for personal reasons, but who definitely deserves to be on this list.

Thank you to this person, whose perspectives are often similar to mine, who reminds me of the good when I need to hear it, who quoted Steven King on drugs when I was sad (I have not found that quote irl tho), and who inspired me to write the texts 'Thought thoughtless thoughts', 'Caught in between two worlds' and 'Language is a playground for the rich', as well as part of 'Butterfly effect' and the entire chapter 'Words, many of them, my heart, my soul'. I am glad that I have met you and I hope we will keep in touch with one another! xo

It remains for me to thank my wonderful readers, and especially the people who spread the word about my work by recommending it or sharing a picture of it on social media.
I see you and I really appreciate your efforts!

My final gratitude goes to the café where I retreat when I want to write without being disturbed.

I now not only have a regular drink there (vanilla chai latte with cinnamon) but also a regular seat.

Thank you, Othello.
(@othello_kaffeebar)

Lilli J Wettke was born in Trier in 2007. In addition to her job as a karate-teacher, she is very interested in psychology, philosophy, poetry and physics.
She is currently a student at a secondary school.
In her spare time she enjoys reading, politics and writing alongside of creating art.
You can find her on social media under
@lilli.wettke and @written.by.lilli.

Lilli J Wettke
Drenched- Love letters I wish I could send you

"So now I am writing down all of those love-drenched
words of mine,
that I would much rather scream out into the world,
say to your godlike face,
right here,
right now,
at this perfect little moment of infinity."